SEO
GUIDE

2017 EDITION
SEARCH ENGINE OPTIMIZATION
GUIDE FOR BEGINNERS

KENT MAURESMO

Copyright

Legal Terms
Disclaimer & Terms Of Use

The information contained in this material (including, but not limited to any manuals, CDs, recordings, MP3s or other content in any format) is based on sources and information reasonably believed to be accurate as of the time it was recorded or created. However, this material deals with topics that are constantly changing and are subject to ongoing changes RELATED TO TECHNOLOGY AND THE MARKETPLACE AS WELL AS LEGAL AND RELATED COMPLIANCE ISSUES. Therefore, the completeness and current accuracy of the materials cannot be guaranteed. These materials do not constitute legal, compliance, financial, tax, accounting, or related advice.

The end user of this information should therefore use the contents of this program and the materials as a general guideline and not as the ultimate source of current information and when appropriate the user should consult their own legal, accounting or other advisors.

Any case studies, examples, illustrations are not intended to guarantee, or to imply that the user will achieve similar results. In fact, your results may vary significantly and factors such as your market, personal effort and many other circumstances may and will cause results to vary.

THE INFORMATION PROVIDED IN THIS PRODUCT IS SOLD AND PROVIDED ON AN „AS IS" BASIS WITHOUT ANY EXPRESS OR IMPLIED WARRANTIES, OF ANY KIND WHETHER WARRANTIES FOR A PARTICULAR PURPOSE OR OTHER WARRANTY except as may be specifically set forth in the materials or in the site. IN PARTICULAR, THE SELLER OF THE PRODUCT AND MATERIALS DOES NOT WARRANT THAT ANY OF THE INFORMATION WILL PRODUCE A PARTICULAR ECONOMIC RESULT OR THAT IT WILL BE SUCCESSFUL IN CREATING PARTICULAR MARKETING OR SALES RESULTS. THOSE RESULTS ARE YOUR RESPONSIBILITY AS THE END USER OF THE PRODUCT. IN PARTICULAR, SELLER SHALL NOT BE LIABLE TO USER OR ANY OTHER PARTY FOR ANY DAMAGES, OR COSTS, OF ANY CHARACTER INCLUDING BUT NOT LIMITED TO DIRECT OR INDIRECT, CONSEQUENTIAL, SPECIAL, INCIDENTAL, OR OTHER COSTS OR DAMAGES, IN EXCESS OF THE PURCHASE PRICE OF THE PRODUCT OR SERVICES. THESE LIMITATIONS MAY BE AFFECTED BY THE LAWS OF PARTICULAR STATES AND JURISDICTIONS AND AS SUCH MAY BE APPLIED IN A DIFFERENT MANNER TO A PARTICULAR USER.

"Do You Want The PDF Version of This Book?"

At the end of this book, I've included a link so you can download the PDF.

Table of Contents

Introduction

SEO is easy! In this updated book, I'm going show you the easiest way to get on the first page of Google. Most SEO agencies will charge you up to $1,000 just to audit your website which is too expensive for most small business owners. In this book, I'll show you how to audit your entire website for free in less than 2 minutes.

My name is Kent Mauresmo. I'm a web designer with a strong focus on search engine optimization (SEO) and search engine marketing (SEM). I'm one of the webmasters and content creators for seocompanylosangeles.us, and many other websites. I'm also one of the authors of the book, "**How to Build a Website with WordPress...Fast!**" If you've already read that book, then you should be familiar with a few of our basic SEO techniques.

In this updated book, I'll show you how to fully optimize your website fast! Follow my step-by-step system and your website will show up on the first page of **Google**, **Yahoo**, and **Bing** too!

In the next image you'll see some results for my keywords in Los Angeles. Los Angeles is the 2nd biggest city in the United States, and "search engine optimization" and "digital marketing" is a very competitive field.

The tiny marker you see next to "seo services", "seo company", and "seo consultant" on my ranking report in the previous image are local results. **Local SEO** is very important because Google will show different results based on your location. I'll teach you how to setup your website to rank in your local city or service area for your main keyword.

After your website is fully optimized, I'll show you where to go to analyze your entire website for free to make sure it's perfect! After you tweak your website's settings, I'll show you exactly how to get backlinks to your website to boost your rankings on Google fast!

Depending on your niche, I can't guarantee that you'll end up on the first page of Google overnight. Should that discourage you? No way! Why not? It's common knowledge that once you're on the first page on Google, you'll usually stay on the first page as long as you continue to maintain your website.

I'm going to expose the truth about SEO. After you read this book, you'll think twice about hiring an SEO company. SEO is not as hard as most people think. It's actually just common sense, and once you know the secrets, **it's easy.**

The techniques you'll discover will <u>boost</u> your website's rankings fast. I feel confident in saying that 90% of your competition will virtually <u>disappear</u> once you apply my **step-by-step system.**

<u>DISCLAIMER</u>: This book may have a few grammatical errors. If you read for style or literary quality, then this book isn't for you. This is a raw guide to show you how to easily:

- Do your own SEO
- Dominate 90% of your competition
- Get on the 1st page of Google, Yahoo and Bing...fast!

<u>What Are Some of The Updates In This Book?</u>

Some of the updates in this book include:

- Alternative keyword research methods
- How to set up your web hosting account for SEO
- Greyhat SEO methods
- Google places and business listings
- New SEO tools
- Updated piggyback methods
- Tiered backlinks (backlink pyramids)

Are you ready? Let's get started!

Chapter 1
Advanced Keyword Research

What are keywords? Keywords are words or phrases that people type into Google to find your business. In this chapter, I'm going to show you how to easily discover profitable keywords for your website.

The **easiest way** to find keywords for your website is by typing your main keyword into Google, Yahoo, and Bing. The search engines will show you related keyword phrases based on user search habits.

I'm going to use the keyword *"dog training"* for this example. In the next image, you'll see that Google has provided some **excellent keywords** that I need to write down.

Searches related to dog training

private dog training **los angeles**	dog **trainer los angeles yelp**
dog **obedience** training **los angeles**	dog **remedy behavioral** training
aggressive dog training **los angeles**	**happy paws** dog training **la**
karma dog training **prices**	**karma** dog training **los angeles**

1 2 3 4 5 6 7 8 9 10   Next

Another way to find keywords for your website will require keyword tools. I'll show you three different tools in this chapter sorted by easiest to use to hardest to use.

<u>Keyword Research Database</u> - <u>https://serps.com/tools/keywords</u>
This is an excellent research tool and as of today, it's still free to use. This tool will show you keywords related to your business, search volume (how many people search for the keyword per month), and "cost per click" data (CPC). CPC data shows you how much advertisers are paying to advertise on Google for a certain keyword.

If advertisers are willing to pay a lot of money for a keyword, then it's a **profitable keyword** for them. Advertisers bid on keywords, so the market sets the price. You can use this information to determine which keywords might be the most profitable for your website.

Below you'll see what some of the results look like.

dog training|

Keyword Search Results

Keyword	Volume	CPC	▼ Value
filter keyword			
dog training	40,500	$2.97	$120,285.00
ahimsa dog training	590	$6.73	$3,970.70
cesar millan dog training	880	$3.00	$2,640.00
bird dog training	720	$2.56	$1,843.20

<u>Ubersuggest</u> - <u>http://ubersuggest.io</u>

With ubersuggest, you can <u>instantly</u> get thousands of keyword ideas from real user queries. Use the keywords to get ideas for your blog posts, or use the keywords for your website's homepage.

Ubersuggest takes your base keyword, adds a letter or a digit to the front of it, and **extracts suggestions** for it. Ubersuggest extracts these suggestions from search engines and video websites like YouTube.

Just enter your main keyword phrase and click the "suggest" button. In the next image you'll see what some of the results look like.

<u>Google Keyword Tool</u> - https://adwords.google.com/KeywordPlanner
Most people show you this keyword tool first, but I'm showing this tool last. Why? Recently Google made a change to this tool. You now have to setup an adwords account with Google to access their keyword tool which requires your credit card information.

A lot of people are annoyed with this change, but Google's keyword tool has always been for adwords advertisers. Google doesn't make any money if you're ranking on the first page for FREE; they want you to pay money to get on the first page. People forget that Google makes money through **advertisements**, so why would they want to help you rank on the first page for free?

If you've used Google Adwords advertising in the past, then you'll have access to this tool. If you never used Google Adwords before, then there's a **90% chance** that they're going to ask you for a credit card. Google may change this later, so you can always check to be sure; but as of right now, that's the current situation.

If you decide to use this tool, you'll be able to **search for keyword ideas**, get historical statistics, and see how a list of keywords might perform for your website. To find the keywool tool, login into your adwords account and click the tab that says "Tools" at the top. You'll see "keyword planner" in the drop-down menu and that's where you need to click.

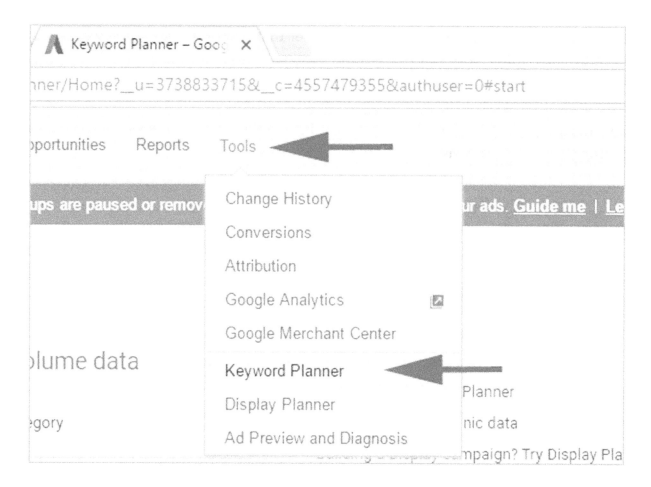

You'll arrive at the keyword planner tool, and you'll be prompted to **enter your keyword phrase**. You'll see a lot of other options too, but most of those options you won't need to worry about unless you plan on advertising on Google.

There's only two options that you *might* want to play with. You'll see an option that says "targeting" and another option that says "keyword filters." If you're a local business, you can use the **<u>targeting feature</u>** to get an accurate count of how many people are searching for your keywords.

If you don't use the targeting feature, Google will display the search volume from all over the world. This could be misleading because you might think 10,000 local people are searching for your keywords, but in reality it might only be 1,000 people.

The "keyword filter" option will allow you to search for keywords based on monthly search volume. For example, you can set a filter that will only display keywords that have at least 1,000 searches per month. This will filter out all the keywords that have low monthly searches.

So enter your **main keyword**, set up targeting and filtering (optional), then click the button that says "get ideas."

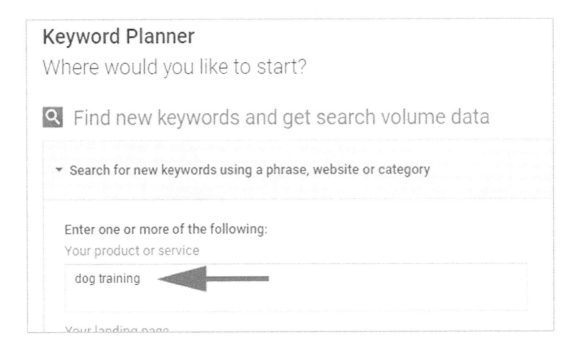

On the next page click the on the tab that says "keyword ideas." You'll see stats for your main keyword and a long list of additional keywords below it.

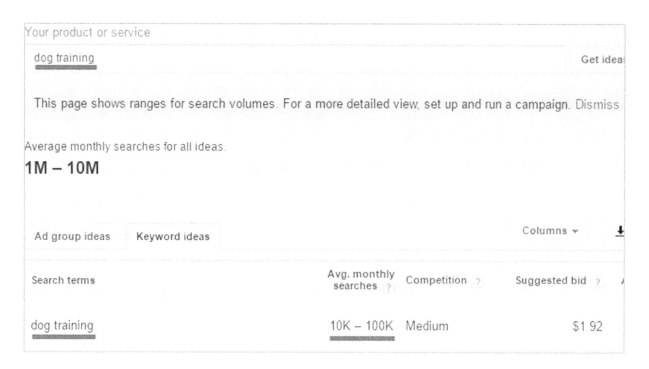

The list of additional keywords you'll see will be **sorted by relevance**. If you want your website to be as relevant as possible, then copy down the keywords in the order they're presented to you.

You can also rearrange the keywords based on monthly search volume, competition, or suggested bid. The competition tab is for advertisers. "High" competition means that a lot of advertisers are bidding to advertise on said keyword. High competition is actually a good sign because that means it's a profitable keyword to advertise on.

Keyword (by relevance)	Avg. monthly searches ?	Competition ?	Suggested bid ?
puppy training	10K – 100K	Medium	$1.20
dog training classes	10K – 100K	Medium	$2.24
dog trainer	10K – 100K	Medium	$2.22
dog obedience training	10K – 100K	Medium	$2.48

The "suggested bid" column will give you an idea of how much advertisers are paying to advertise on Google. The dollar amount you see is only a suggestion. The real advertising cost is usually a lot higher than the dollar amount shown. Advertisers will pay more than the suggestion to get better placement on Google's search engine. You can use that information to decide which keywords will be profitable for your website.

You can write down the keywords you like on a sheet of paper, or just click the "download" option. Google will give you **800 keyword ideas** for each keyword you search for. You can download those keywords into an excel file and sort through them in excel if that's easier for you.

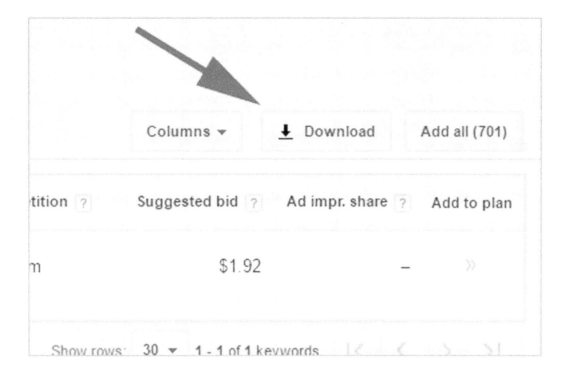

Tips When Choosing Keywords

Choose long tail keywords to rank faster on Google. A long tail keyword has at least 3 words in the phrase i.e. "*dog training classes.*"

You also want to also choose "buyer keywords." A buyer keyword phrase would be something like "*dog training video course*" because the user is looking to **pay** for a dog training course.

Now you know how to easily find profitable keywords for your business! To keep it simple, put together a list of **10 keywords** that you want to rank for and focus on those keywords only.

Summary & Action Plan

Type your main keyword into Google, Yahoo, and Bing and look at the related search terms.

Keyword tools to use:

- https://serps.com/tools/keywords
- http://ubersuggest.org

- https://adwords.google.com/KeywordPlanner (may require credit card registration)

Put together a list of 10 keyword phrases that you want to rank for, and that's it! In the next chapter, I'll show you how to **analyze your list** of keywords to see how competitive they are.

Chapter 2
Keyword Analysis

In this chapter, I'm going to show you how to easily analyze your keyword list. You'll want to analyze your keyword list for a few reasons:

- See what Google is ranking for the keyword (videos, listings, etc.)
- Check for fortune 500 companies
- Check for small business owners
- Look for a lot of Google paid advertisements

To get started, just enter one of your keywords directly into Google. Your "buying keywords" are the most important, so I suggest that you start with those first. As an example, I'm going to insert the keyword "**dog training courses**" into Google. Anyone searching for this keyword phrase is obviously looking to purchase a course, so it's a perfect keyword.

After you click the "search" button, usually the first few results you see are paid advertisements, and you'll see an **green icon** that says "Ad." If you don't see any advertisements then that's not a good sign. Fortunately, there are plenty of advertisements for this keyword so we'll continue.

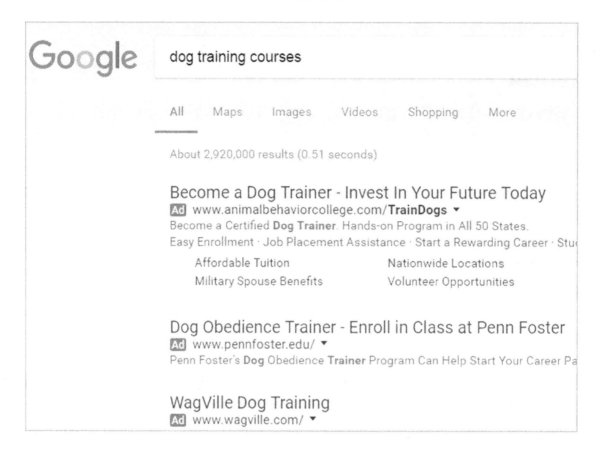

A keyword without any advertisements *usually* means that it's not profitable, or the keyword is copyrighted. For example, one of my clients has a website that sells Instagram "likes" and followers. The word "Instagram" is **copyrighted**, so even though that's a profitable business, you'll rarely see any Google advertisements based around that keyword.

Once you're past the advertisements, you'll see the **organic search results.** The organic search results are sorted by relevance and are based on Google's algorithm.

The first thing you want to look for are **fortune 500 companies** and **huge franchises**. If you see a lot of well known franchises in the organic search results, then you might want to move on to another keyword on your list. But for the keyword "dog training courses", I only see two franchises; PetSmart and Petco. PetSmart has position #1, and Petco has position #6.

As I look through the organic listings, the rest of the search results look like small business owners. I usually click on all the websites to **size up the competition**. You can tell a lot about a company by the way their website looks.

If your competition has a homemade looking website, then chances are they made it themselves. If they made the website themselves, then they're probably doing their own SEO too. What makes them so different from you? **Nothing.** You can bump them right off the first page.

I don't see any YouTube videos for this keyword which is interesting. I had to go all the way to page 5 to find a YouTube video in the organic search. Google *will* actually rank a YouTube video for this keyword, but the video I found on page 5 **wasn't optimized correctly.**

I also noticed that the websites listed were located all over the country. A lot of people will be looking for something local which is why Google prompts you to use the keyword *"dog training courses near me"* or *"dog training courses online."*

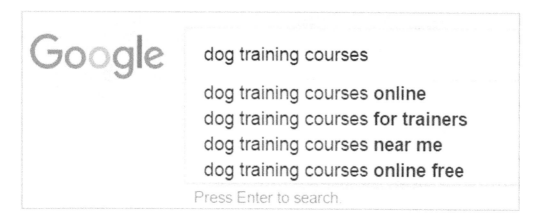

That's important feedback from Google. If you offer a local dog training course, then you should adjust your keyword to *"dog training courses + your city."*

If you offer an online dog training course, then you can adjust your keyword to *"dog training courses online."* The adjusted keyword may have a lower search volume, but it doesn't matter. When someone lands on your website, they're more likely to buy from you because you're offering **exactly** what they're looking for.

I think the keyword "dog training courses" is easy to rank for, so I'd add it to my list. Now just repeat this step for each keyword phrase that you want to rank for. **You**

must analyze your competition first to make sure you're not trying to rank for an almost impossible keyword phrase.

If every single search result on the first page of Google is a fortune 500 company, then you might want to choose another keyword from your list.

Tools To Make It Easy

I realize that my process to analyze keywords might be complicated to some people. I have a solution for you to make the keyword analysis process easier.

You can use a free SEO Toolbar available at: https://moz.com/products/pro/seo-toolbar

I never use this toolbar because I don't like to over analyze my competition. But if you want to really dissect your competition, then I suggest that you use the MOZ toolbar. The Moz toolbar is currently free to download.

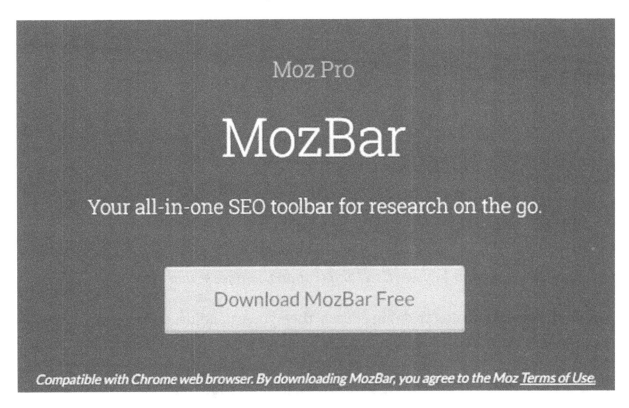

Once you install the MOZ toolbar, you can scan through Google's search results and this tool will analyze the pages for you at a glance. You can visit their website for more information.

You can also use a keyword analysis tool called "*Market Samurai*" if you feel like going into SEO ninja mode. They have a video on their website too showing you how the tool works here: http://www.marketsamurai.com

I personally don't like keyword analysis tools because they don't make sense to me. For example, **some keywords** will produce results from Yelp, Yellow Pages, YouTube videos, Facebook pages, and Amazon product pages.

When a keyword analysis tool sees these results, they'll tell you that it's an impossible keyword to rank for because they'll think you're trying to compete with those popular websites. The tool doesn't understand that anybody can create accounts at all those sites (i.e. YouTube, Yelp, Facebook) and just rank the individual page.

Summary & Action Plan

- Manually type your keyword into Google. If you see a lot of fortune 500 companies on the first page for a keyword, then you know that it will be a difficult keyword to rank for. Just because a keyword is difficult **doesn't mean it's impossible**. It might take you 6-12 months to rank for that specific keyword, so just set realistic expectations.
- If you notice a lot of small business owners on the first page for a particular keyword, then **you can compete immediately.** A lot of small business owners don't hire SEO companies, so there's a good chance that they're on the first page by accident. It's also important to note that a lot of SEO companies aren't that good at SEO. Just follow my advice and you'll bump them off the first page.
- If you notice a lot of Google advertisements for a keyword, then that's a **good sign**. As I mentioned earlier, advertisers will only advertise on a keyword that's making them a profit. The more advertisements you see for a keyword, the better!
- Keyword analysis tool: https://moz.com/products/pro/seo-toolbar

- Keyword analysis tool: http://www.marketsamurai.com
- Update your keyword list based your research.

In the next chapter, I'll show you how to set up your web hosting and domain names to rank higher on Google, Yahoo, and Bing!

Chapter 3
SEO & Web Hosting

In this chapter, I'm going to show you how to choose a domain name and web hosting that will improve your SEO.

Domain Names

When choosing a domain name, try to choose a domain that includes your keyword phrase. For example, let's say I own a dog training company and I decided to call my company "Mauresmo's Pooch Center." People love to name their businesses after themselves, but you need to **be smart** when choosing your domain name.

Let me ask you a question. Which domain name do you think would be better for my dog training company?

- www.Mauresmos.com
- www.MauresmosDogTraining.com

Obviously the second domain name is way better, but most newbies will choose the first one. Your domain name doesn't have to match your business name exactly. You should build your website on a domain name that includes at least **one of your keywords** because you'll rank higher on Google, Yahoo, and Bing.

In my example, I would buy **both** domain names, but I would build my website on *MauresmosDogTraining.com*. When the website is finished, I'd set up a redirect so that *Mauresmos.com* forwards to *MauresmosDogTraining.com*.

That would be the best way to setup my domain names. Why? Because my website's content will on the **keyword optimized domain name** which will rank higher on Google, Yahoo, and Bing. But since I setup the redirect, I can add the simpler domain name, *Mauresmos.com*, on my business cards and other marketing material.

When you register your domain name, register it for **at least 2 years**. If you have the budget to register your domain for 5 or 10 years, then do it. The longer your domain name is registered, the more trusted you'll seem to search engines.

Most people that register a domain name for only a year build a quick website to try to make money. If the website doesn't make money within the first couple of months, most people abandon the website. A lot of spammers also register domain names for only a year because they're only going to spam the website and it's going to get blacklisted anyways.

Only a real company will register a domain name for a few years because they plan on growing their business. So if you're a real company, prove it. Register **new domain names** for at least two years.

Fast WordPress Web Hosting

Some web hosting companies have special hosting designed specifically for WordPress. For example, if you go to GoDaddy's website, you'll notice that they have "Managed WordPress Hosting."

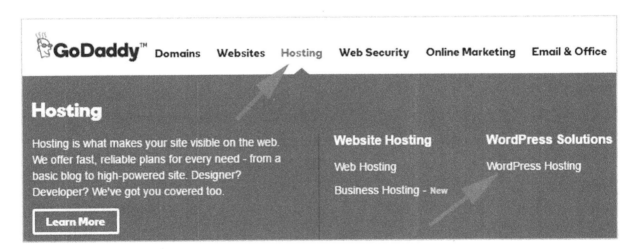

Managed WordPress hosting is faster than normal web hosting for a lot of reasons. Managed WordPress hosting has certain limitations (1 - 5 websites per hosting account) and restrict certain WordPress plugins that are known to cause problems with WordPress. The restrictions create an **ideal hosting environment** which allows your website to move really fast.

Most people have **basic** shared hosting accounts. The basic shared hosting plan offers unlimited websites and unlimited everything else, so it seems like a good deal. But if you're sharing an hosting account with someone that builds 20 websites and installs 500 faulty plugins, then that can affect your website's performance.

Managed WordPress hosting limits the amount of websites that you can build, and limits the amount of traffic you can receive. The limitations are **more than reasonable** for the average business owner, and anyone planning to do something shady won't even bother with managed WordPress Hosting. Perfect!

All your files are automatically cached with managed hosting, so your website loads very fast. There's no need to install complicated cache plugins that never work or break your website. I personally think managed WordPress hosting is the way to go if you want a **simple, fast**, and **secure** hosting solution.

Everyone knows that a slow website is bad for SEO because it's a poor user experience. So based on my experience, managed WordPress hosting **fixes 90% of the speed issues** right away.

SEO is challenging enough without the added stress of trying to figure out how to speed up your sluggish website. It doesn't matter how good your SEO is or even if you're on the first page of Google. If your website is slow, people will leave your website before they get a chance to look at your products and services.

SSL Certificates

SSL stands for Secure Sockets Layer. An SSL certificate ensures that all data passed between the web server and browsers remain private. You'll know if a website is secure because the domain name will start with ***https://.***

Websites that process credit card information are required to have an SSL certificate. What if you don't process credit cards? Do you still need an SSL certificate? If you have a **contact form** on your website, then you're still collecting personal information (name, email address, phone number, address, etc.) A lot people won't enter their personal information on an unsecure website.

SSL certificates will help you rank higher within the search engines because it's a user friendly experience. Secured websites are **considered safe** which protects the user.

Most people don't know this, but if you try to **<u>advertise on Google</u>** and your website isn't secure; they may reject your website. Unsecure websites that ask users to enter personal information are considered phishing websites to Google.

A **phishing website** (sometimes called a "spoofed" site) tries to steal your account password or other confidential information by tricking you into believing you're on a legitimate **website**. You don't want search engines to think you're a phishing website.

If you want to advertise on Google and your landing page asks for a name and email address; you're going to need an SSL certificate. Google will also require that you have a "**privacy policy**" and "**terms & conditions**" page explaining how you plan to use the information you're collecting.

Even if you never plan to advertise on Google, this is very important feedback from Google. Google is essentially telling you how they differentiate a real company from a fly-by-night business.

Go to any dating website or social network like Twitter, Facebook, or Instagram and you'll see a **disclaimer** before you sign up with your email address. The disclaimer usually says something like "By signing up, you agree to our terms and conditions, privacy policy, and cookie use" and the page will be secured with an SSL certificate.

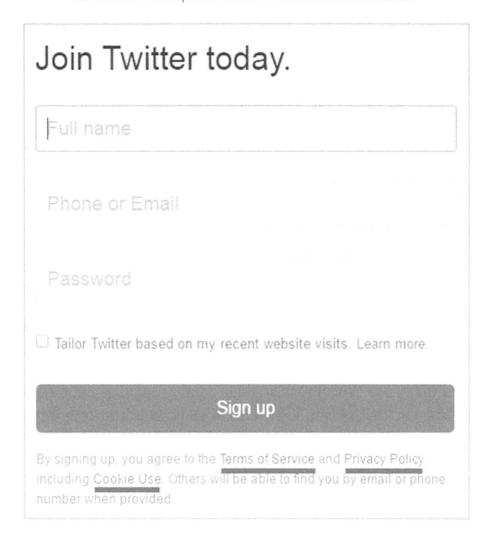

Some web hosting companies will give you an SSL certificate for free the first year. I know **GoDaddy offers a free SSL certificate** for the first year, then it's $69/year after that. An SSL certificate isn't necessary, but it's definitely something to consider.

Summary & Action Plan

- Choose a domain name that includes your keyword
- Choose web hosting optimized for WordPress: Bluehost & GoDaddy
- Install an SSL certificate

Chapter 4
WordPress Setup & SEO Plugins

In this chapter, I'm going to show you how to:

- Optimize your WordPress settings
- Install and setup WordPress plugins for SEO

What if you don't have a self-hosted WordPress site? **That's perfectly okay**.
Most of the settings I'm going to show you can be setup or edited on pure HTML websites, Joomla, Magneto, Wix, Drupal, Squarespace, plus more.

Most websites today use WordPress as their content management system because it's easier to use. For that reason I'm going to show you how to edit the setting in WordPress, but you can make similar edits on the platform that you're using.

How To Optimize Your WordPress Settings

Log into your WordPress dashboard and navigate down to the "settings" tab. Within the settings tab, you'll see an option for "General" settings. Click on that option and you'll see a section asking you for your "site title" and your "tagline."

Enter your **main keyword phrase** into the "site title" section. In the "tagline" section enter your main keyword first followed by a short description of your website. For the site title, keep the text under 60 characters. For the "tagline" keep the character count under 155 characters. You can use a website like http://www.charactercountonline.com to count the characters.

Why should you do this? Sometimes Google will extract your site title and description from this general settings area and show it in Google search results. You want to keep the title under 60 characters and tagline under 155 characters so the full text will show in Google search.

Later I'm going to show you which SEO plugin to install to setup a unique title and description for every page; but it's **important** to setup the general settings with your keywords as a backup.

By default, the general setting area usually says something like "Just another WordPress Blog" for the site title. If you don't change the general settings, Google *might* index your website in the search results displaying the phrase "Just Another WordPress blog." This happens to a lot of my clients.

Some of my clients websites get indexed in Google using a title and description that they don't recognize. After I log into their website, the problem is with their general settings

The next settings that you'll want to check is your **permalinks**. You'll find the "permalinks" option under the settings tab as well. Just click on "settings" and click on the word "permalink."

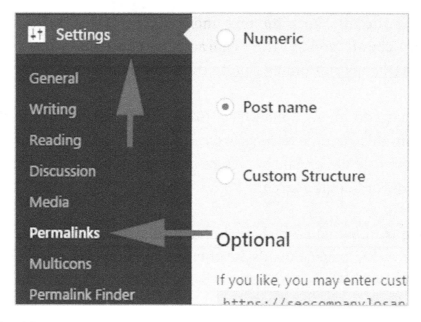

Select the checkbox next to the option that says "Post name." This is **the best** permalink structure to for SEO.

The default permalink structure doesn't give search engines information about your blog posts. The "post name" structure will create permalinks that have the same title as your blog posts and articles.

For example, if I decided to write an article on my website entitled "How to Blog":

- The *default* permalink structure will create a link like this:
read2learn.net/?p=123
- The *Post Name* permalink structure will create a link this:
read2learn.net/how-to-blog

The "post name" permalink structure allows humans and search engines to read your keywords. If search engines can read your keywords, they'll know what words to rank your website for in Google.

WordPress Plugins To Install

Install the WordPress plugins below to improve your on-page SEO:

- **All In One SEO Pack** by Michael Torbert
- **Google XML Sitemaps** by Arne Brachhold
- **WP Sitemap Page** by Tony Archambeau
- **WP Smush** by MPMU DEV

To install these plugins, navigate down the plugins tab, click "*Add New*", search for the recommended plugins, click install, then activate!

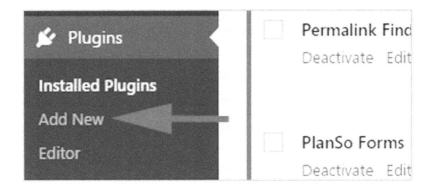

Install all the plugins and I'll show you how to set them up right now. The first plugin we'll setup is "All in One SEO Pack"

All in One SEO Pack

On the top left of your WordPress dashboard, click the *All in One SEO* tab to adjust the homepage settings. For this plugin, you'll need to enter information for the:

- Home Title
- Home Description
- Home Keywords

For the **"Home Title"** section, enter your most important keyword **first**, then enter the name of your company second. Why should you do this? Google looks at your home title (title tag) to determine what your entire website is about.

If your website is about dog training, then enter the phrase "Dog Training" first. Make sure to keep your home title **under 60 characters** so Google will display the whole thing. If you "stuff" your home title with a lot of keywords (keyword stuffing) or make it longer than 60 characters, Google might ignore your title tag and replace it with their own.

Here's a few ways to write a proper home title using your keyword first:

- Dog Training | Kent Mauresmo's
- Dog Training Los Angeles – Kent Mauresmo's
- Dog Training Classes At Kent Mauresmo's

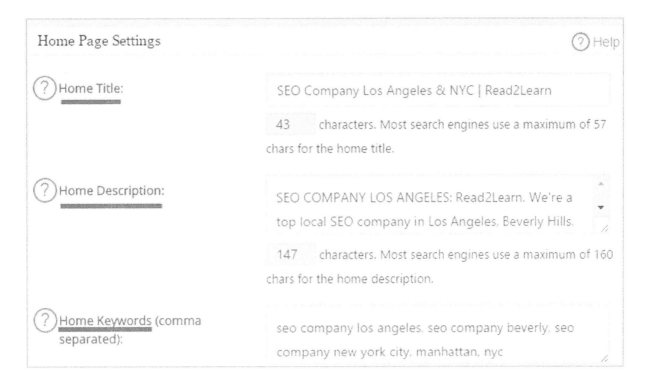

For the **"Home Description"** (description tag) enter your most important keyword first and then describe what your website is about. Once again, the search engine gives a lot of weight to the first few words in your homepage description.

You can use your keyword twice in the home description, but don't "stuff" your description with the same keywords over and over again. Stuffing keywords in your description tag is unprofessional, and you run the risk of getting penalized by Google.

The **"Home Keywords"** (keyword meta tag) section is where you can enter a few keywords that are relevant to your homepage. If you don't see this keyword section within the plugin, that means you have to enable it. If you scroll down the plugin page, you'll see a section that allows you to enable the "keyword settings."

Keyword Settings

(?) Use Keywords: ● Enabled   ○ Disabled

(?) Use Categories for META
    keywords: ☐

You only need to enter a **few keywords** into this section. Spammers have abused the meta keyword tag to the point that Google claims they don't even consider it as a ranking factor anymore. So just enter a 5 – 10 related keywords and you're done. If you add 100 keywords there, it's not going to help you and it's probably going to look like spam to the search engines.

What else does the "*All in One SEO*" plugin have to offer?

If you scroll down the page, you'll see additional options, but you can leave most of those settings the way they are. There are a few updated settings on this plugin that'll make life easier.

For example, you'll notice that this plugin has a "**Webmaster Verification**" area where you can enter your verification code for *Google Webmaster Tools*, *Bing WebmasterCenter*, and *Pinterest Site Verification*.

Webmaster Verification   (?) Help

(?) Google Webmaster Tools:

(?) Bing Webmaster Center:

(?) Pinterest Site Verification:

The *Google Webmasters Tool* will give you detailed information about your website's performance. Before the *Google Webmasters Tool* can give you information about your website, they'll give you a verification code to enter on your website to **verify your ownership**. The *All in One SEO* plugin gives you a specific area to enter the verification code instead of searching through your website's HTML code to find the correct spot.

The *All in One SEO* plugin also has an area for you to enter your "Google Plus" profile information, and your Google Analytics ID. Once again, this will **make life easier for you** so you don't have to manually enter HTML code on your website. When you're finished, just scroll all the way down and click the "Update Options" button to save your settings.

If you're not using WordPress, you can manually edit all these settings in the HTML code. If you didn't create the website yourself, ask your web designer to make the changes for you.

Google XML Sitemaps
Under the settings tab, look for the link that says "XML-Sitemap." This will probably be the last item within your settings tab. Click the link to go to your Google XML Sitemap settings.

The only thing you need to do with this plugin is click the link that says "Build sitemap" or "Build my first sitemap."

This plugin will automatically build a sitemap for you. An **xml sitemap** will help search engines find all the pages on your website and index them with Google.

Result of the last ping, started on December 18, 2016 6:07 am.

The URL to your sitemap index file is: https://seocompanylosangeles.us/sitemap.xml.

Google was **successfully notified** about changes.

Bing was **successfully notified** about changes.

Notify Search Engines about your sitemap or your main sitemap and all sub-sitemaps now.

If you encounter any problems with your sitemap you can use the debug function to get more information.

If you like the plugin, please rate it 5 stars or donate via PayPal! I'm supporting this plug

Alternatively, you can create a sitemap for free online and upload it to Google. You can create the sitemap here: https://www.xml-sitemaps.com. After your sitemap is created, you can submit it to Google using their webmaster tool here: https://www.google.com/webmasters.

WP Sitemap Page
An **HTML sitemap** allows site visitors to easily navigate your website. It's a bulleted outline of your websites navigation. The anchor text displayed in the outline is linked to the page it references.

Site visitors can go to the sitemap page to **locate a topic** they are unable to find by searching the site or navigating through the site menus. Using the sitemap, search engines become aware of every page on the site, including any URLs that are not discovered through the normal crawling process used by the search engine.

POSTS BY CATEGORY

- Category: best local seo company
  - SEO For WordPress Training Videos
  - Testimonials & Reviews
  - Best Local SEO Company: Los Angeles
- Category: best seo company
  - SEO Tool Coming Soon
  - SEO Tools: Do You Need Them?

Sitemaps are helpful if a website has dynamic content, is new and doesn't have many links to it, or contains a lot of archived content that is not well-linked.

After you activate this plugin, **create a page** on your website, name the page "Sitemap", and paste this shortcode on the page: [wp_sitemap_page]. When you're finished, publish the page and link to the page on the footer of your homepage.

If you're not using WordPress, that's not a problem. You can create the sitemap manually by listing your most important pages.

WP Smush

If you have a website with a lot of images or large images, they can slow down your website. WP Smush is a plugin that **compresses your images** as you upload them. If you're installing the plugin for the first time, you can use it to compress images that you've already uploaded to your website.

To find WP Smush, click on the "media" tab on your dashboard, and then click on the "WP Smush" link. You'll see an option to "bulk smush" all your current uploaded images. After your images are compressed, this plugin will show you how much space you saved by compressing your images.

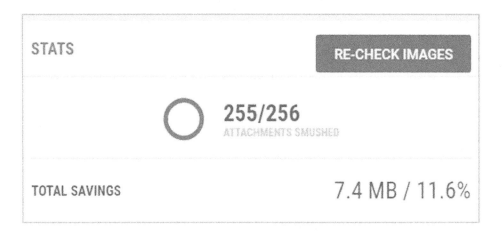

If you're not using WordPress, just make sure that you compress and/or optimize your images before you upload them to your website. There are many free resources that you can use such as:

- http://optimizilla.com
- https://tinypng.com

If those websites are no longer free by the time you read this book, just perform a Google search for "optimize images." There's a lot of free resources that will compress your images for you.

Even if you're using WordPress, you should get into the habit of compressing and resizing your images first before you upload them to your website.

Summary & Action Plan
Install the WordPress plugins below:

- All In One SEO Pack
- Google XML Sitemaps
- WP Sitemap Page
- WP Smush

In the next chapter, I'll show you how to optimize your homepage.

Chapter 5
Homepage

In this short chapter, I'm going to show you how to optimize your homepage for SEO. When you setup your homepage, you want to make sure that your **exact keyword** is placed in your:

- Title tag
- Description tag
- H1 tag
- H2 tag
- H3 tag

You already setup your title tag and description tag using the "All In One SEO" plugin. In this chapter, I'm going to show you how to set up the H1, H2, and H3 tags on your **homepage**.

The first thing you need to understand is the proper structure for SEO. Your homepage should have only **one** H1 tag, **one** H2 tag, and the rest of the tags can be H3 - H6. So here's the setup:

- H1 tag = heading of page (one per page)
- H2 tag = subheading of page (one per page)
- H3 - H6 tags = subsections (multiple per page)

```
<h1>Heading 1</h1>
<h2>Heading 2</h2>
<h3>Heading 3</h3>
<h4>Heading 4</h4>
<h5>Heading 5</h5>
<h6>Heading 6</h6>
```

These tags are **very important** for SEO, but most web designers completely ignore these tags. Most websites have multiple H1 and H2 tags on the homepage. A lot of web designers use H1 and H2 tags to make the font bigger on certain areas of your homepage, but that's a problem.

If you have ten H1 tags on your homepage, then you're communicating to search engines that your homepage is focused on **ten different things**. There's no way to know where your tags are (H1 - H6) without looking at the code of your website.

You can **scan your website** using the tools below to reverse engineer your website. After you scan your website, these tools will show you which phrases on your homepage are your H1, H2, and H3 tags. Find the corresponding phrases on your homepage to identify your tags.

Here's a few tools that you can use below. They're not free anymore, but they'll allow you to scan your website **at-least once for free**:

- http://seositecheckup.com
- https://www.site-analyzer.com
- https://www.woorank.com

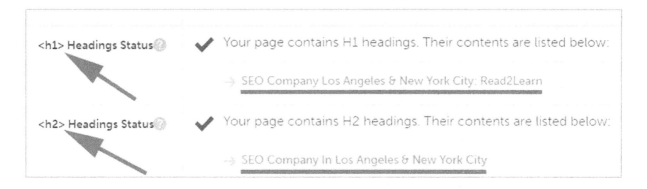

After you scan your website, you'll probably notice that you have multiple H1 and H2 tags on your homepage. If you're capable, change the unnecessary H1 & H2 tags into H3 & H4 tags. If you don't know how to make the changes yourself, **don't panic!** You can hire someone from Upwork.com or Fiverr.com to make the changes for you for less than $30 USD.

After you make the changes, make sure that you **add your keyword** to your H1 tag and your H2 tag. Also if you're using WordPress and you created your website using a template, it's important that you don't update your template after you make the changes. If you're using a template and you click the "update" button to get the lastest features for your theme, you'll reset all your heading tags and you'll have ten H1 tags again.

When setting up the tags on your homepage, it's important that you **don't skip any tags** either. For example, if you're going to have an H5 tag on your page, then you'll need to have an H1-H4 tag on your page too that leads up to the H5. This may sound confusing, but it's not. All you have to remember is this:

- H1 tag = heading of page (**one per page**)
- H2 tag = subheading (**one per page**)
- H3 - H6 tags = subsections (multiple per page is okay)
- Don't skip any tags. Set your tags in order.

Word Count

Depending on your website's theme, you may or may not be able to add a lot of text to your homepage. If you're able to add a lot of text to your homepage, then add **2,000 words** or more describing your product or services. Search engines love content, so the more content you have, the better.

Optimized Content

As you're writing content on your homepage, you should use your exact keyword within the **first few sentences**. You should also **bold**, *italicize*, or <u>underline</u> your exact keyword within the first few sentences.

You don't want to stuff your homepage with keywords because it will look like spam. To be safe, use your exact keyword only **2-4 times** on your homepage, then use the related keywords from your keyword lists.

Your exact keyword should be found in your "anchor text" too. Anchor text is a word or phrase that's a **clickable hyperlink**. Simply highlight your keyword, select the "insert link" option on the toolbar, then enter the URL to your homepage. Now your keyword is a clickable link the redirects users to your homepage.

Link To Your Blog & Sitemaps on Your Homepage

Most people have blogs on their website, but a lot of people don't link to the blog on the homepage. You need to make sure that you add your blog to your **menu bar** so search engines and users can find it easily.

Your blog page is usually updated more than any other page on your website. Search engines are always looking for new updated content which is why blogs rank higher in the search results. Your blog is one of your most important pages, so make sure it's easy to find.

You also need to link to your **XML Sitemap** and your **HTML Sitemap** on your homepage. Why? The <u>XML Sitemap</u> tells the search engine about the pages on your site, their relative importance to each other, and how often they're updated.

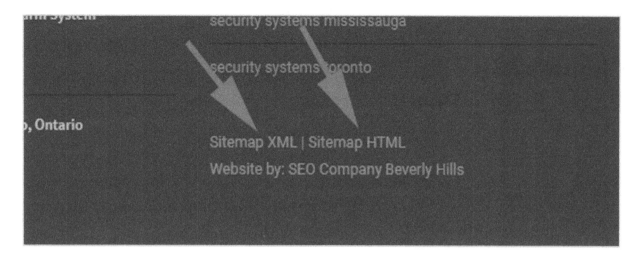

<u>HTML sitemaps</u> are designed for the user to help them find content on the page. This **helps visitors** and search engine bots find all pages on the site.

As you can see, both sitemap pages are **important** so it's important that you link to those pages on your homepage. You can link to your sitemap in the footer of your website so it's not intrusive.

You should have already setup and installed the Google XML sitemap plugin, and the WP sitemap plugin. All you have to do is link to both of those sitemap pages.

<u>Summary & Action Plan</u>

- Add one H1 tag to your homepage (include main keyword)
- Add one H2 tag to your homepage (include main keyword)
- Hire help for tags if needed (upwork.com, fiverr.com)
- Add 2000+ words to homepage if your theme allows for it
- Use your exact keyword within the first few sentences
- Bold, underline, or italicize your main keywords
- Use your exact keyword as anchor text on your homepage
- Use your exact keyword only 2-4 times on your homepage
- Link to your blog on your homepage
- Link to your XML sitemap on your homepage
- Link to your HTML sitemap on your homepage

Chapter 6
Pages & Blog Posts

Writing search engine optimized articles for your website is **a lot easier** than you think. Some people spend hours trying to pick the best titles for their articles, and that's a complete waste of time.

The best titles for your articles are within your **keyword list** that you saved earlier. If 12,000 people per month are searching for the keyword phrase "**buy graphic design art**", then you should use that exact keyword phrase as the <u>title</u> of your article for three reasons:

- WordPress and most website templates uses your title as an <u>H1 tag</u>. Search engines look at your H1 tag to determine what your entire article is about.
- You'll increase your chances of showing up on page #1 of Google when your H1 tag matches a search query.
- People are also more inclined to click on an article from Google when it's an exact match their search query.

<u>Permalinks</u>
After you enter a title for your page/blog, your permalink should automatically populate below the title. You'll notice that your permalink is an exact match to your title.

If your permalink doesn't match the title of your article, just click the "edit" button next to your permalink. Edit the permalink to make sure that it matches your title exactly. (*See next image*)

Search engines will scan your permalinks, so you need to include your keywords there. If your **permalinks match the title of your article** (H1 tag), then you'll get a bump above your competition.

H2 & H3 Tag

The next thing search engines look at is your **H2 tag**. To find the H2 tag option, you have to click the <u>formatting drop down list</u> on your toolbar. After you click the drop down list, you'll see something that says "Heading 2" which is the H2 tag.

If you don't see this formatting drop down list, then you need to click the icon that says "<u>toolbar toggle.</u>" WordPress hides these formatting options by default.

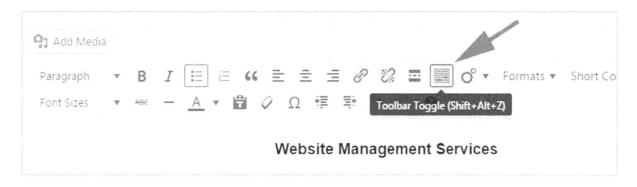

To use the H2 tag correctly:

1) Type the <u>same keyword phrase</u> that you have in your title and permalinks.

2) Select the text by dragging your mouse across the keyword phrase to highlight it.

3) Click the formatting toolbar and select "Heading 2" which is the H2 tag.

You'll notice that the H2 option makes the text bigger and bold. You can also add an extra word or date at the end of the keyword phrase if you like. I usually add an extra word or phrase at the end of my keyword phrase in the H2 tag so it doesn't look like I repeated the title for no apparent reason.

For example, if my main keyword phrase is, *"buy graphic design art"*, I'd set my H2 tag to say one of the following:

1) **Buy graphic design art** in 2017
2) **Buy graphic design art** – Exclusive Discounts
3) **Buy graphic design art** for cheap!

As you can see, the main keyword phrase is still there and you're just expanding on it. This looks good to search engines and even better to your **readers**.

Do the same thing with the **H3 tag**. Use the H3 tag at least once in your article as a subheading to break up your text. For example, if your keyword is *"buy graphic design art"*, you could use a H3 subheading somewhere in your article like this:

Buy Graphic Design Art for Cheap at:

- **Amazon.com/link-to-your-prodcuts**
- **Ebay.com/link-to-your-products**
- **DeviantART.com/link-to-your-prodcuts**

First Paragraph

Your first paragraph should have your keyword phrase at least once. The best way to do this is by asking a question or making a statement. For example:

1) "Are you looking to **buy graphic design art** for cheap? We've got you covered!"

2) "**Buy graphic design art** for 50% off during the month of February!"

Make sure to **Bold** and <u>Underline</u> your keyword phrases. Search engines will acknowledge these phrases as important and give you extra "juice" for these keyword phrases.

It's not that hard to write a sentence that makes sense using your keyword phrase. Just make sure that you don't stuff your keywords into a paragraph if it doesn't make sense.

If your article doesn't make sense, then people will bounce off your page. That basically means that people will click on your link from Google, stay on your page for a couple seconds, and then hit the "back arrow" to go back to Google.

<u>If you have a high "bounce rate" then Google will bounce you off the first page of the search results</u>. Google wants to provide their users with relevant and useful information. So if people keep bouncing off your page, then obviously your content isn't relevant to what people are looking for.

<u>Keyword Density</u>

A lot of SEO guys are really big on keyword density. SEO companies have figured out a certain percentage of times that they *think* your keyword phrase should show up within an article.

Keep in mind that you're supposed to write for your **READERS** and not for search engines. Don't randomly insert keywords into a paragraph just to meet a keyword density percentage. I personally think that's going overboard.

Just <u>sprinkle</u> your keyword throughout your article and make sure it reads well. You need to impress your readers because they are more important. If your readers like your article, then they'll share it on Facebook and Twitter, and Google will notice that. As a reward, Google will move you ahead of your competition.

<u>Last Paragraph</u>

The last paragraph is very important. Make sure that you include your keyword phrase at least <u>one more time</u> in the last paragraph. Just make sure that it seems natural so it's not obvious to your readers what you're doing.

Using the same example, "buy graphic design art", I would probably start off my last paragraph like:

"***Buy graphic design art*** *from us today and save 50% off the retail price! If you have a special request, please feel free to contact us using the contact form. You can also contact us using our toll free 800 number. We have over 15 years experience, and all of our clients are happy customers. Order from Amazon or contact us to request a custom order!* "

Lastly, you'll want to add some **anchor text** at the end of the article that points back to the <u>same article</u>. Anchor text is just a hyperlink that contains your keyword phrase. For example:

<u>Buy Graphic Design Art</u> ← That's **anchor text**. (see next image for another example)

might want to take a minute and think again. It doesn't matte good of a programmer you are or how much you know abou long as you want your website to be a success, you need to incorporate the aid of a website management company. The are some reasons why you might want to incorporate the aid <u>website management</u> company.

More Time to Grow Your Business

By incorporating the aid of a website management company gain the freedom and time to focus on the core aspects of y business. Imagine you start a website which needs updates

<u>Upload Optimized Images</u>

You need to add images to all your blog post and articles. Images break up the text and make your articles a lot easier to read.

You <u>shouldn't</u> steal pictures from Google Images. Everybody does it, but you shouldn't because you might run into copyright issues.

You can download images **legally** a few different ways:

1) Buy royalty free images: http://www.istockphoto.com
2) Use screenshots from your computer like I'm using in this book.
3) Do a Google search for "free royalty free images."
4) Ask users from http://www.Flickr.com or http://www.DeviantArt.com if you can use their images in your articles. A lot of people will agree, and they'll just ask for credit for the image.

Before you upload your images to your website, you need to **rename them** with the same title as your article. Save your images to your desktop, right click on the image, and select the "Rename" option.

If you have more than one image, you can still use the same keyword phrase for **all your images** by adding a number or word at the end. For example:

- Buy graphic design art.
- Buy graphic design art 2016.
- Buy graphic design art now.
- Buy graphic design art at an discount.

When you upload your images to your website, the optimized image name will automatically populate into the "Title" box. Now copy and paste that keyword phrase into the **alternate text** box, **caption** box, and **description** box.

You should alternate the keywords so it's doesn't seem like spam to the search engines. If you **look at the screenshot below**, you'll see that I'm using the keyword "website management" in all the sections, but I'm building around the keyword so it's not spam.

URL	https://seocompanylosangeles.us/wp-cc
Title	website management services
Caption	website management service Los Angeles
Alt Text	affordable website management
Description	local website management company

All in One SEO Pack Blog Settings

After you finish uploading your images, scroll down the page and you'll see the "*All in One SEO Pack*." There's a section for a **Title**, **Description**, and **Keywords**. Whatever information you enter into this plugin will be the same information displayed on Google search.

Since we already optimized the blog post, you just need to copy the same information from your article into this plugin. So for the *title*, enter in the title of your article. For the *description*, enter your **main keyword first**, add a hyphen, and then enter the first 2 sentences from your article. For the *keywords* section, enter 3-5 keywords using your main keyword first.

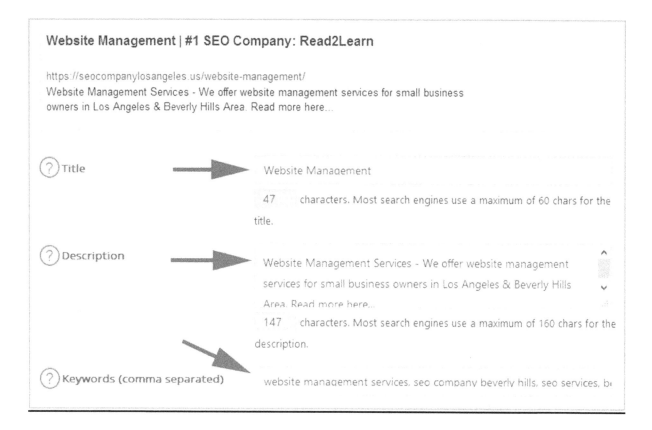

Categories & Tags

On the right column, you'll notice a section that says *categories.* A lot of people ignore this section, but it's very important.

You only need to add one category per article, but you can add more. If you're not sure how to categorize your articles, look at your keyword list and use those as categories.

Below the category section, you'll see a box that says "**Tags**." You can add multiple tags to your articles, but try to limit yourself to five tags so it doesn't look like spam. You should add the title of your article as one of the tags, and refer to your keyword list if you want to add additional tags.

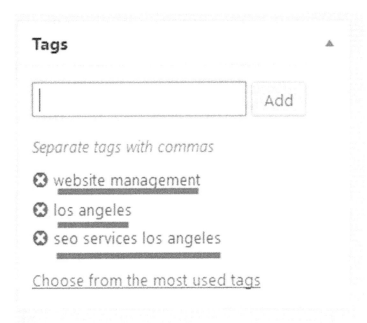

Below the *tag* section, you'll see a *"Featured Image"* section as well. Upload your main image there, and make sure that you use the same "image optimization" tips that we've discussed earlier. Done!

Tag Cloud Widget

Within your WordPress dashboard, navigate to the "widgets" section. You should see a widget for "tags" or "tag cloud." You should add this widget to your sidebar because it will **help search engines** determine what your website is about.

When search engines crawl your page, they'll see your tag cloud and follow the links to all your articles. Tag clouds are **great for SEO**.

Summary & Action Plan

- The H1 tag is the title of your article
- Add your keyword to the H1, H2, and H3 tags within your article
- Make sure your keyword is in your permalink
- Add your keyword to the first paragraph of your article
- Bold, underline, or italicize your main keyword
- Add your keyword to the last paragraph
- Add your keyword to the images (title, alternative tag, description)
- Add your keywords to the "tag" and "categories" section.
- Customize the "All In One SEO" plugin for each article
- Setup the "tag cloud" widget on your website

If you're not using WordPress, you can easily make these changes in the HTML code of your website. If you didn't design your website, you can ask your web designer to implement these changes for you.

Everything I'm showing you can be done on any type of website. WordPress just makes it easier because you don't have to know HTML code to make the changes.

Chapter 7
Analyze Your On-Page SEO For Free

Use Traffic Travis to review your on-page SEO. Traffic Travis is a free software that you can download from their official website here: www.traffictravis.com

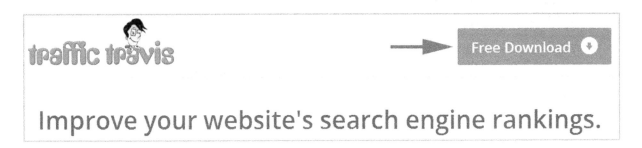

You'll have to register your name and email to download the product. Use your **real email** address because they're going to email you a "product key" that you'll need to access the tool.

After you launch the software and **enter the product key**, the program will start to play a video showing you how to use the software. You can close that video for now and watch it later. That same video will start again every time to open the software. After you close the video, you'll be presented with three options:

- Watch Video
- Create New Project
- Let Me Play

Choose the "Let me Play" option, and then click the tab on the top left that says "My Site."

After you click the "My Site" tab, another video will open showing you how to use the "My Site" feature. You can watch that video if you'd like, but I'm going to show you how to use it now. On the top left, click the button that says "import pages." Traffic Travis will ask you to **import your sitemap** file. Your sitemap file will look like this:

- **YourDomainName.com/sitemap.xml**

After you enter your sitemap, scroll down and click the box that says "Import Keywords from Meta Keywords." When you're finished, click the "OK" button.

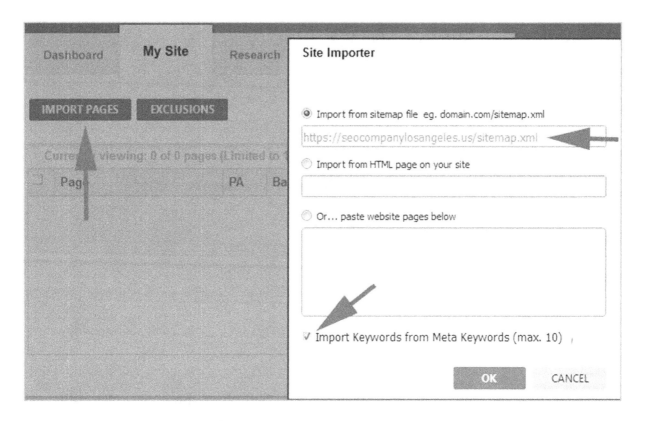

After you click "OK" Traffic Travis will start to analyze your website. After it's finished, you'll see a column that says "Page Warning."

Within that *page warning* column you'll see a "number" if you have any on-page SEO problems. Click on the number to find out how you can fix your on-page SEO. Below is an example of an error I found on one of my websites.

Now that I see what's wrong, I can go back to my website, make the changes **myself**, and then come back to Traffic Travis and analyze my website again to make sure the problem is fixed.

Summary & Action Plan

Analyze your entire website for free using Traffic Travis. Using traffic travis, you need to:

- Click on the "my site" tab
- Click on "import pages"
- Enter your sitemap URL (**YourDomainName.com/sitemap.xml)**

The only thing holding you back from getting on the first page of Google now is **backlinks** to your website.

In the next chapter, I'll go into more detail about backlinks and off-page optimization.

Chapter 8
Off-Page Optimization

After you optimize your homepage, blog posts, and articles; you'll need to create backlinks to your website. A backlink is a **link on another website** that directs users back to your website. For example, I wrote an article about "WordPress Plugins"on my website, and I included a link to *WordPress.org* in my article. That counts as a backlink for the *WordPress.org* website.

There are a lot of ways to get backlinks to your site. The most popular ways are:

- Blog Commenting
- Article Marketing
- Forum Posting
- Social Bookmarking
- User Profiles, etc.

Blog Commenting

When you leave a comment on someone's blog, sometimes you'll see an option to enter your website's URL too. When you enter your website's URL, your "display name" on the comment changes into a clickable link that points back to your website.

This is my **LEAST favorite way** to get backlinks for a few reasons:

- You have to <u>read</u> the article first if you plan to leave a valid comment.
- Most comments are held for <u>moderation</u>, so it's up to the website's owner if your comment will show up or not.
- The website owner can edit your comment and <u>remove your link.</u>
- Posting comments all day takes <u>too much time</u>. Time is your most important asset.

Leaving blog comments is good, but I wouldn't waste a lot of time leaving comments if you're **only** trying to build backlinks.

Article Marketing

Article marketing is a really great way to get backlinks to your website. The downside is that it can be time consuming to write 100 different articles and post them to 100 different article directories.

The truth is that nobody does this anyway. Most people write an article **once** and then pay someone to _spin_ it and submit it to multiple article directories. When I say "spin" the article, I simply mean mixing the words around in an article to make it seem as if it's a different article.

Spinning an article is "greyhat" SEO because a spun article is **technically** a "low quality" article. Even if the article is manually spun so it makes sense when someone reads it, it's still a "grey area" because you're essentially uploading the same article all over the internet for the sole purpose of getting backlinks.

You won't get "penalized" for duplicate content unless you upload duplicate content on your actual website. Also, duplicate content is NOT actually "penalized" anyways. Think about it, Google and article directories simply **don't need** the same article 100 times. So Google won't index duplicate content (because they already have that content) and article directories will reject an article with duplicate content because they already have the content too. So duplicate content isn't actually penalized because it's never accepted to begin with.

Now if an entire website is filled with duplicate content or spun articles, then the entire website might get penalized or de-indexed because the website doesn't have anything unique for Google to index.

Google wants to provide users with unique results. It wouldn't make sense if the first page of Google had the same article 10 times. That's the only reason why Google and article websites do not like duplicate content. So if you submit the **same exact article** to 100 different article directories, then the directory _might not_ approve your article.

If by luck your articles are approved by article directories, Google might not index those article into their search results to keep their search engine free from duplicate content.

So you actually have three choices:

1) Write unique articles to submit to article directories (whitehat SEO)
2) Manually spin one of your current articles (greyhat SEO)
3) Pay article writers to write unique articles for you (whitehat + $$$)

You can use websites like **Upwork.com** or **Fiverr.com** to find article writers, or people to help you spin articles. Just be careful with Fiverr because you get what you pay for. A lot of users on Fiverr use automated/spammy techniques that are useless. You might want to give them a **sample** project first to check out their work. If it looks good, then you can give them your main project to work on.

You can actually outsource the entire article writing and submission process. Just **don't go overboard** when outsourcing article marketing or any other backlinking services.

If you pay someone to submit 2,000 articles so you can get 2,000 backlinks within 24 hours, then you're asking for trouble.

2,000 backlinks within 24 hours will **not look natural** to Google and they *might* penalize you...maybe. The way Google can penalize you is by pushing your website to the back of their search results, or just removing your website all together from their search engine.

You're better off paying someone $20 to **manually submit** your article to 20 article directories rather than paying someone $5 to automatically submit to 2,000 directories. One of my favorite article directories is hubpages.com.

I recommend that you sign up for **Hubpages** and manually submit your articles there yourself. It's good to know how these article directories work and what kind of articles they accept. When you write your articles, use the same SEO strategies that you used on your WordPress website.

Remember to use "*anchor text*" with your main keyword phrase when you post your links on article directories. Most article directories will make this easy for you by asking for your **URL** and then the **Display** text.

If an article directory requires HTML code for anchor text, just use the template below and replace the *URL* with your website, and the text "*Wikipedia*" with your keyword phrase:

<a href="http://en.wikipedia.org/wiki/Main_Page">Wikipedia</a>

Forum Posting

This is another of my **least favorite** options to get backlinks to your website. I personally don't like forums because they're usually filled with people passing along poor advice, but you can get quality backlinks there.

When you sign up for forums, you can set up a profile which allows you to add a link that points back to your website. Most forums will also allow you to set up a signature similar to an email signature. When you leave a comment on the forum, your website's link will show up under your posts. (*See next image.*)

You have to be an active user of forums to get multiple backlinks pointing back to your website. If you like forums, then this is perfect for you! If not, then underline outsource this project to someone else.

There are some outsourcers that'll set up multiple forum profiles for you and leave a couple comments on the forums. You can use Upwork, Fiverr, or whatever other outsourcing website that you feel comfortable with. Just don't use Freelancer.com because a lot of people have complaints against that website including me.

Social Bookmarking

This is my favorite way to get backlinks. Social Bookmarking websites allow you to share your favorite websites with everybody on the internet. Popular social bookmarking sites include:

- www.stumbleupon.com
- www.digg.com
- www.delicious.com
- www.diigo.com
- www.reddit.com
- www.folkd.com, and a lot more.

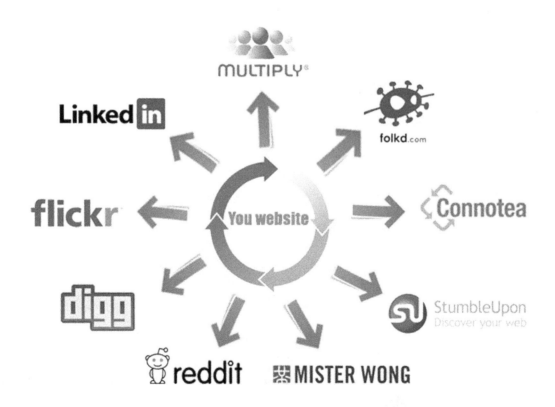

When you register with social bookmarking websites, you have to use those websites correctly or you could get banned. If you only bookmark pages from your website, then it's considered "self promotion." Self promotion is the fastest way to get your website banned from *some* social bookmarking communities.

Your social bookmarking accounts should **look natural** just like your bookmarks within your web browser. Every time you bookmark your articles, you should also bookmark 5-10 other websites as well.

You need to sign up for all the social bookmarking websites to see how they work. **This is not a waste of time** for multiple reasons:

- Social Bookmarking websites have a very high page rank with Google.
- When you set up your profile, you can add your URL for a backlink.
- You can upload your logo to help people get familiar with your brand.
- You need to know how these websites work if you decide to outsource this task. The only way you'll know how these websites work is to sign up for them and use them.

It only takes about **10-15 minutes** to bookmark your website to about 12 of these social bookmarking websites. That includes bookmarking additional websites to make your accounts look natural.

Each website has a toolbar that you can download to make the bookmarking process faster. I personally recommend using the "AddThis" toolbar which combines all the popular bookmarking sites into one easy to manage toolbar.

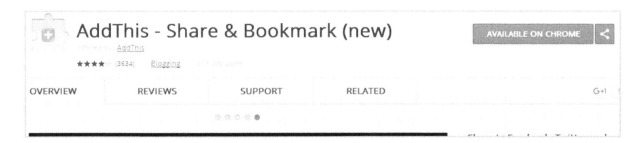

To find this toolbar for the Firefox Mozilla browser:

1) Go to https://addons.mozilla.org
2) Type "addthis" into the search box.
3) Look for the Orange Square with the (+) symbol inside of it, and click the "*Add to Firefox*" button.
4) Restart your browser and set up the social bookmarking websites that you'd like on the toolbar.

If you're using Google Chrome, you can search for the extension on this page: https://chrome.google.com/webstore/category/extensions

If you want to take Social Bookmarking to the next level, you should:

- Bookmark any article that you left a blog comment on.
- Bookmark all your articles that you posted to article directories.
- Bookmark every forum page that you left a comment on.
- Bookmark any and every page that displays your websites link.

When you bookmark a page that displays your link, Google will find your link **faster** and count it as a backlink. Also by bookmarking the page, you're making that page more important in Google's eyes which will also make your link on that page more important.

Profile Accounts

Creating profile account are fun. Profile accounts are created at websites that allow you to upload a photo and a link to your website. This is a great way to get backlinks, and even better for branding.

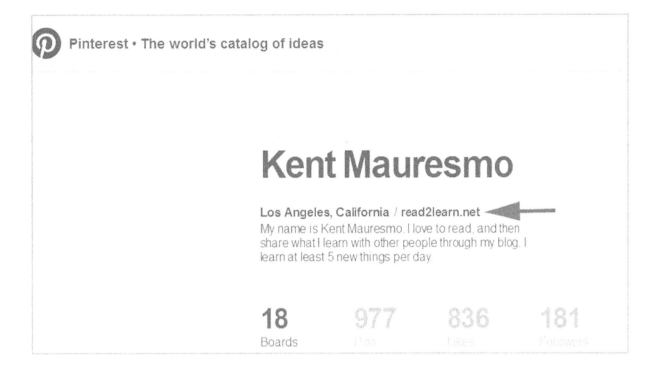

If a website is considered important to Google, then you want to affiliate yourself with that website. The **easiest way** to do this is to set up a profile with these websites and upload your logo and your website's address. You can do this yourself, have someone in your office do it, or outsource this task to Upwork.com.

An example of a profile account that allows you to **display your website** is Twitter. Search engines will notice this backlink, and people that visit your Twitter profile will see your link and click it if they want to know more about you.

The goal is to create profile accounts at websites that are considered important by Google and that have a lot of authority. I found the easiest way to do this is to go to www.alexa.com, click the "*Top Sites*" tab, and scroll down the list to see which websites will allow you to create profile accounts (*see next image.)* Obviously you don't want to create a profile account on a porn website, but everything else should be fine.

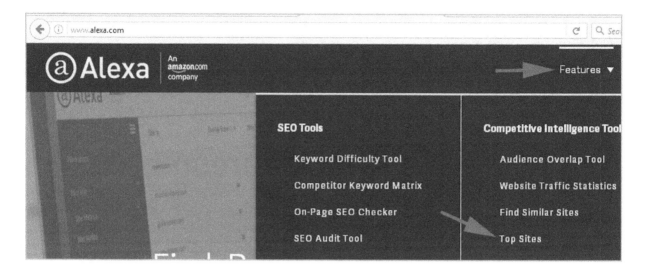

Heres a few websites that you can create profile accounts on:

1) https://profiles.google.com/me
2) http://www.facebook.com/pages/create.php (Facebook Fanpage)
3) http://amazon.com
4) http://www.flickr.com
5) http://blogger.com
6) http://pinterest.com
7) https://www.tumblr.com
8) http://wordpress.com (Not to be confused with WordPress.org)
9) http://www.linkedin.com
10) http://digg.com
11) http://www.slideshare.net
12) http://www.myspace.com
13) http://www.stumbleupon.com
14) http://www.warriorforum.com
15) http://www.deviantart.com
16) http://youtube.com
17) http://www.nytimes.com
18) http://www.reddit.com
19) http://www.livejournal.com
20) http://vimeo.com
21) http://dailymotion.com
22) https://about.me

Most people don't like to create profile accounts because they're too lazy, but that's their loss and your gain. Some people argue that some of these websites are "no-follow" which basically means that the backlink doesn't count, but I disagree.

Google looks at **all** links pointing to your website and it's supposed to be mixed with do-follow, no-follow, blog comments, links from articles, links from videos, and profile links especially from authority websites.

Like I said earlier, if you have links from multiple **authority websites** pointing back to your site, then Google will have no choice but to consider you an authority website as well.

On the other hand, if you have a lot of <u>spammy links</u> pointing back to your website, then Google will consider you a spammy website too and penalize you. It's better to have 100 authority backlinks compared to 10,000 spammy backlinks.

I believe that you should create these profile accounts yourself to **make sure it's done right**. You should also upload your company logo and actively use these websites once or twice a month.

After you create these profile accounts, don't forget to use *Social Bookmarking* websites to bookmark the page that displays your websites link. This will help the search engines index your links **faster** and your profile pages will start to show up in Google search.

If you type "Kent Mauresmo" into Google, you'll see profile accounts from plenty of authority websites on the first page.

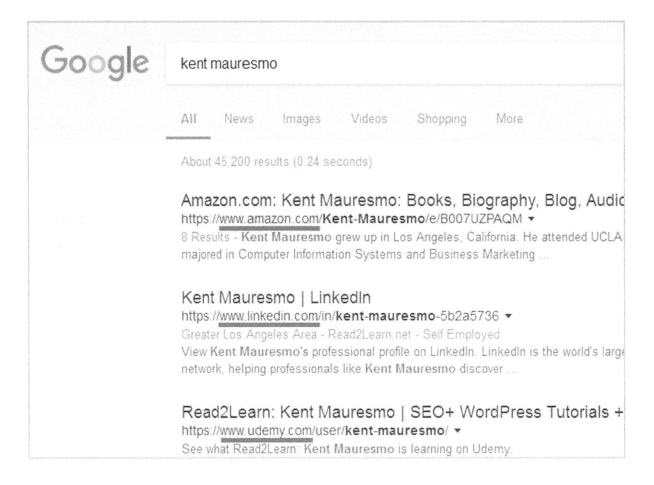

Summary & Action Plan

Manually build backlinks to your website using:

- Blog Commenting
- Article Marketing
- Forum Posting
- Social Bookmarking
- User Profiles, etc.

To get started, you can find quality websites to get backlinks from at: http://www.alexa.com/topsites.

Chapter 9
Tiered backlinks (Backlink Pyramids)

Tiered backlinks (backlink pyramids) are when you **build backlinks to your backlinks.** This sounds confusing, but it's really simple. Other websites that link directly to your website are considered **tier 1** backlinks. Websites that link to the tier 1 pages are considered **tier 2** backlinks.

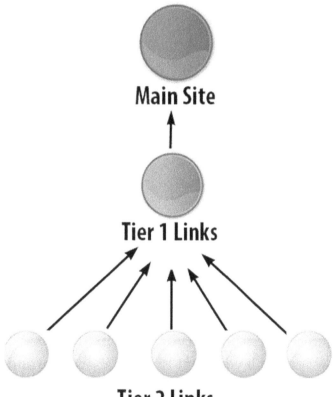

Main Site

Tier 1 Links

Tier 2 Links

For example, let's say I created a *Facebook Fan Page* that links directly to my website. That would be considered a "Tier 1" backlink because it links directly to my website.

Next, let's say I created three articles on HubPages that link to my Facebook fan page; that's considered "Tier 2" links because HubPages links directly to my Facebook fan page instead of directly to my website.

You should create tiered backlinks for a few reasons:

- Help Google find your tier 1 backlinks
- Make your tier 1 backlinks more important
- Protect your website from lesser quality backlinks

A whitehat backlink pyramid will consist of **quality backlinks** on tier 1 **and** tier 2. So if your tier 1 backlink are on Facebook, and your tier 2 backlinks are on a **quality article directory** like HubPages, then it's a whitehat pyramid.

A blackhat/greyhat backlink pyramid is *almost* the same. A blackhat pyramid consist of a lot of **low quality backlinks on tier 2**. For example, my tier 1 backlink would still be on an authority website like Facebook, but I would create 2,000 backlinks on tier 2 using a lot of spun articles on auto approve article directories. The spun articles aren't linking directly to my website, they're linking to my Facebook fan page, so my website is technically safe.

Facebook isn't going to get penalized because I sent 2,000 backlinks to my fan page; Facebook probably has billions of backlinks from all over the place. The only thing that will happen is that **Google will find my Facebook fan page faster** due to all the links pointing to my page and index it.

The entire point of tiered backlinks is to create a "push" for your tier 1 links. Your tier 1 links should only come from **authority websites**. Your tier 2 links can come from wherever you want, but if you want to be 100% ethical and "whitehat", you can use social bookmarking websites for your tier 2 links. (Diigo, Digg, Folkd, Delicious, Google+, Reddit, etc...)

Summary & Action Plan

Build backlink pyramids to **help Google find all your backlinks**. Your tier 1 backlinks are links that point directly to your website. Your tier 2 backlinks point to the tier 1 backlinks.

Your tier 1 backlinks should always consist of **high quality**, authoritative, and relevant websites. Your tier 2 backlinks can consist of lesser quality backlinks, but if you want to be 100% safe and whitehat, use social bookmarking websites for tier 2 backlinks. Done.

Chapter 10
Boost Your Rankings With RSS Feeds

Do you know what an RSS Feed is? If not, it's that orange icon you see on a lot of websites (*see next image.*) Internet users can subscribe to your website via these RSS Feeds, and have your articles sent to their eReader device or email. If you don't have an RSS feed installed on your website, you can get one for free at https://feedburner.google.com

Once you have an active feedburner account, you can submit your feed URL to feed directories. You can search Google to find websites that accept RSS feeds, but a few good ones are:

- http://www.feedage.com
- http://www.specificfeeds.com
- http://www.plazoo.com
- http://www.rssmicro.com
- https://feedly.com/i/welcome

Just look for a button that says "submit feed" on all of these websites. Some feed directories you'll have to register for, and some other directories will allow you to submit your feed anonymously without creating an account.

After you submit your feed, the title of your articles will become **clickable anchor text** that points back to your website. That's why it's very important that you always title your articles correctly because it will always be used as a clickable link which is **anchor text**.

Also, don't forget to build backlinks to your RSS feed pages. I know a lot of this seems tedious, but if you want to make it to the first page of Google, then you have to work for it.

There are only <u>ten free spots</u> on the first page of Google, and depending on your market, you could be competing with millions of other web pages. Only the business owners that are willing to go above and beyond will make it to the first page of Google and stay there.

<u>Summary & Action Plan</u>

- Submit your RSS feed to feed directories
- If you don't have an RSS feed, you can create one at:
  <u>https://feedburner.google.com</u>
- Build backlinks to your RSS feed pages.

Chapter 11
Get Your Backlinks Found By Google, Fast!

Google will only find about 10% of your backlinks. For every 100 backlinks you build, Google will only find 10. If Google doesn't find your backlinks, then the backlinks won't count for your website, and you won't move up in Google's rankings. You can help Google find all your backlinks fast by creating tiered backlinks as mentioned earlier; or you can use **indexing services.**

Indexing services uses a wide range of techniques to make search engines aware of your backlinks. If you **build quality backlinks**, you'll increase the chances of your backlinks getting indexed by Google. If you create low quality spam backlinks, then Google won't index your backlinks even if you use an indexing software.

Here are three services that you can use to help Google find and index your backlinks:

- http://onehourindexing.co
- http://linklicious.co
- http://www.indexification.com

All of the indexing websites above cost less than $19/month. You **must** create tiered backlinks or use an indexing service for your backlinks.

Most people miss this important step and they wonder why their website isn't **moving up the rankings.** I know some people that spend hours writing articles, submitting to directories, and creating profile accounts; but it's all for nothing if Google doesn't find those pages that contain your backlinks.

Tiered backlinking is confusing to some people, so you'll need to invest in one of the software's mentioned above. I personally use "**One Hour Indexing**" and it works great.

I recommend that you only use these services to get your tier 1 backlinks indexed. **Don't import pages from your actual website** into the indexing software. WordPress is already setup to "ping" search engines when you publish new content to your website.

Chapter 12
Track Your Rankings

This chapter will be short, but it's very important. You need to **track your rankings** to make sure your SEO efforts are working for your business.

Every business is different, so an **SEO strategy** that works for one business might not be as effective for another business. For example, if you own a local restaurant, backlinks from social media websites might be enough to get you on the first page of Google, Yahoo, and Bing.

What if you own an insurance company? Welcome to the big leagues! You'll need backlinks from facebook, twitter, pinterest, press release websites, PDF websites, private blog networks, PR9 domains, 301 redirects from aged domains with authority, site-wide links, Youtube, Vimeo, DailyMotion, forums, profile accounts, blog comments, article directories, everywhere and **lots of on-page content.**

How do you know which backlink strategy is working the best? Just **use one type of backlinks for the month** and track your rankings for that month. For example, for one month you can focus on building backlinks using only video websites like Youtube.

Before you start building backlinks, sign up for Accuranker here: https://accuranker.com.

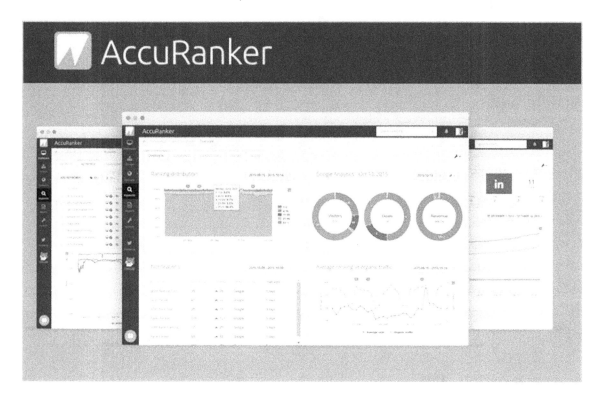

Accuranker is a simple and affordable solution to **track your rankings** on Google and Bing. They offer a free trial so you can test it out first, and there's no credit card required. You can track the rankings of up to 150 keywords for $19/month.

You can track your rankings on mobile devices, **track your competition** for the same keywords, set target goals, have automated reports sent to you, and click a single button to update the rankings for all your keywords. The rankings are automatically updated once daily, but you can refresh your rankings as many times as you want.

You don't have to use accuranker; there's other software that you can use. I use accuranker because it's **user-friendly** and affordable, but you can use any software you want. Whatever software you use, you'll need to track your rankings to see what's going on.

If you're not going to **track your progress**, then don't even waste your time doing your own SEO. I'm serious, you have to keep track of what you're doing to make sure it's having an **positive effect** on your website.

If what you're doing isn't working, then try a different backlink strategy. Most importantly, don't give up on SEO because you think it's not working. You can get backlinks 100 different ways, so just keep testing until you find the **perfect formula** for your business.

All the strategies I'm giving you work, but you might not need all of them. You're supposed to work smart, not hard. Focus your efforts on the SEO strategies that **work the best** for your website.

I know some people that write 3-5 blog posts per day. Their entire SEO strategy is **content creation** (search engines appreciate new original content) and they're constantly moving up the search results and getting thousands of visitors per day. They don't even worry about backlinks because their readers are sharing the content on other blogs and social media.

Summary & Action Plan

- Track your rankings using: https://accuranker.com
- Build one type of backlinks per month and track your rankings with accuranker. This will help you identify which type of backlinks are working and not working.
- If the backlinks you're using are improving your rankings, then keep doing that but also start on to the next type of backlinks. You need link diversity.
- If you start a new backlink campaign and your rankings drop, don't panic. Your rankings can drop for no reason at all, just make a note of what you were doing just to be safe.

Chapter 13
Piggyback Method

Search engines like to mix up their search results with **YouTube** videos, social media websites like **Pinterest**, products from **Amazon**, and images. So if you want to improve your chances to rank for a keyword, you need to optimize your content and syndicate it to all these popular websites.

For example, to help <u>rank your Amazon book</u> on Google, Yahoo, and Bing you have to:

1) Title your book using the exact keyword phrase you're trying to rank for, and include your keyword phrase again in the description section for your book.
2) Once your book goes live; social bookmark your book's page and set up an article marketing campaign with links pointing back to your book.

PDF Sharing Websites

Scribd.com is a website that allows you upload and share PDF documents. You can utilize Scribd to **build backlinks** to your website, build brand awareness, and get to the first page of Google. You can do this easily by:

- Creating a new article using Microsoft Word.
- At the top of your document enter your website address.
- Click the "save as" option, and select "**PDF**."
- When you save your document, don't forget to use your main keyword phrase as the file name.

Now all you have to do is log into your Scribd account at <u>www.scribd.com</u> and upload the PDF document. When they prompt you for the title of your article, use your main keyword. When you enter your description, use your main keyword **FIRST** and then enter your description (just like your website.)

If want the PDF document to rank, build backlinks to the **Scribd document** using social bookmarking and article directories.

You can repeat this process using other popular document sharing websites like:

- www.issuu.com
- www.flii.by
- www.pinterest.com
- www.4shared.com
- www.academia.edu
- www.slideshare.net

You can also perform a Google search for "PDF sharing websites" to get a list of more websites that you can submit your PDF documents too.

YouTube Tips

YouTube is a little tricky. You need to have a lot of "views", "likes" and "comments" on your video for Google to consider your video important and rank it. Not to worry because you can outsource this task to somebody for $20-$30

You don't need a master's degree in video editing to upload a simple promo video to YouTube. Just go to www.animoto.com and you can create a professional slideshow in about 10 minutes. You can also record a screencast (record your computer screen) using a simple software like http://www.techsmith.com/camtasia.html.

When you upload your video to YouTube, use your main keyword phrase in the title, description and tags. You can also place your website link in the description too, but make sure that you use "**http://**" in front of your web address so the link will be clickable.

Also, **enter your main keyword phrase FIRST** and then enter your website's URL in the description. There are some other tricks in regards to YouTube too, but that's an entire book in itself that we'll probably write later. But if you submit your YouTube videos to social bookmarking sites, you'll increase your chances of the video showing up in the search engines.

Even if your video doesn't get to page #1 of Google, creating backlinks on YouTube is still a good **back linking strategy** and you'll get some decent website traffic. YouTube is owned by Google, so you're "keeping it in the family" when you utilize YouTube.

Q&A Websites

"Question & Answer" websites like **Yahoo Answers, Wiki Answers,** and **Quora** are great websites for your business. These types of websites are great because:

- You get to set up a **profile account** and include your website's address and logo.
- You can answer a lot of questions which is great for branding your company.
- You're allowed to include links in the "resource" section when you answer questions. This is a **good opportunity** to post links back to your website or your PDF documents that'll answer a specific question in more detail.

Have you ever typed a question into a search engine and the top results were from **Yahoo Answers?** That's exactly why you need to sign up for an account with Yahoo Answers and use it for a couple days.

Millions of people visit Yahoo Answers looking for answers to questions. If people keep seeing your company logo pop up and you're leaving **quality answers**, people will eventually visit your website.

If you have a good website with more useful answers, then people will **link to your articles** and probably share your website on Facebook and Twitter.

There are allegedly hundreds of SEO secrets, tricks, and tactics to help you jump to the first page of Google. Ironically, the best way to get to the front page of Google is to help people solve their problems. When you help people, they'll say good things about you and recommend you to their friends by passing along your websites link. The more people you help, the more people you'll have sharing your website. That's exactly how websites like Facebook became popular. Facebook didn't have an SEO strategy. Instead, Facebook provided a quality service that people liked, and they became popular by word of mouth.

I only bring this up to remind you to always put your readers first. Some people go overboard with SEO and forget that there are real people on the other end of these computers.

Your articles can be fully optimized from beginning to end, but if your content is poor then:

- People will bounce off your website.
- People won't recommend your website to their friends.
- You'll make people mad for wasting their time.
- Google will remove your article from page #1 because of your bounce rate.
- You'll have to build backlinks yourself *forever* because no one will naturally link to your website.

So make sure that you have a good balance when it comes to SEO. Always write your articles for the people first and search engines second.

Chapter 14
Google Places & Business Listings

Business listings are **very important** when it comes to SEO. The business listings on Google, Yahoo, and Bing are displayed before the organic search results.

A lot of people will only contact the first few businesses they see on the business listings. Why? Because people are lazy and the business listing gives them **all the information they need**. Business listings allow people to instantly see the name, address, phone number, and business hours of multiple businesses without clicking on anything.

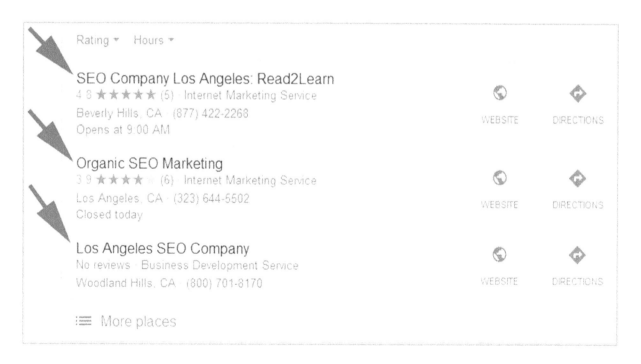

Google used to show 5 - 7 business listing on the first page, but now they only **show 3 listings**. A lot of business owners are upset that Google only shows 3 business listings now, but my response is, "What do you expect?"

I tell people all the time that Google isn't in the business of helping people advertise their business for **free**. Google wants you to give them all your money to pay for advertisements. Google is a business, not a charity.

Yahoo and Bing still show 5 - 7 business listings on their first page, so **don't ignore Yahoo and Bing**. Everybody doesn't use Google; there's a lot of people that use Bing, like me.

Here are the websites to submit your business listings:

- https://www.google.com/business (Google)
- https://www.bingplaces.com (Bing)
- https://www.aabacosmallbusiness.com/local-listings (Yahoo)

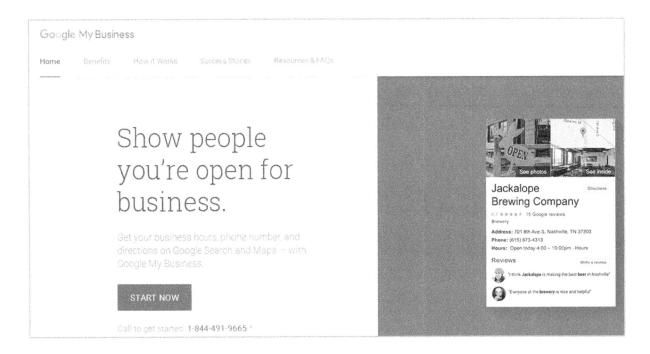

To set up your account, you'll need to have a valid **business address** and **phone number**. Don't submit just any address because they're going to send a postcard with a pin-code that you'll need to verify/activate your business listing.

If you work from home, you can use your home address. If you don't want to enter your home address, then set up a **virtual office**.

Sometimes you'll have to verify your phone number depending on where you decide to setup your listing. An automated system might call your phone and give you a **pin-code**, so a live person has to pick up your phone. If you use an automated voice attendant to pick up your business phone to route your calls, then you'll never get the pin-code and you'll go in circles forever.

If you want to increase the chance of your listing showing up on the first page, **use your keyword in your business listings**. When you use your keyword, it has to make sense because your business listing will go through an approval process. If you've followed everything I've stated from the beginning of this book, then you'll be fine.

If you recall earlier in this book, I made up a fake dog training company called "Mauresmos." The name "Mauresmos" doesn't mean anything to search engines, so I said it would be better to purchase the domain name "MauresmosDogTraining.com."

Now when I set up my business listings, I can legitimately name my listing "Mauresmo's Dog Training" which includes my main keyword. No red flags will be raised because my domain name (and even my logo) will match my listings. Done.

You'll also need business "citations" from other reputable sources. The more citations you have, the more likely your business listing will show up on the first page of Google. **A business citation is simply having your business listed on another reputable business directory**. That's why you should setup your business listing on Yahoo and Bing too.

It's also important to make sure that your address and phone number match wherever you list your business. If your business information doesn't match, then you won't move up the rankings because Google doesn't want to add your business to the first page if your information is possibly inaccurate.

Summary & Action Plan

- Submit your business information to Google, Yahoo & Bing!
- Use your keyword within your listing (if it makes sense)

- Keep your business listing information the same across all directories
- Build backlinks to your business listings because they contain your web address. (tier 1 backlinks, remember?)

Conclusion

You should now have a better understanding of SEO. Every strategy that I've recommended has worked for me and still does. **You won't have to worry** about Google changing their algorithms because it will not affect you negatively if you follow this guide.

Every time Google has updated their search engines, our blog posts and articles have actually **moved up** in the search engines. The reason for all the Google updates is to remove "Splogs."

A "splog" is a blog which the author uses to promote affiliated websites to increase the search engine rankings of associated sites. Splogs are also used to simply sell links and ads.

So if you're trying to rank a splog on the first page of Google, then you're going to run into a lot of problems every time Google changes things around. But if you operate a legit website that provides a real product or service, then you'll be fine. You've already taken the first step by reading this book. The second step is to **put what you've learned into action.** If you still have questions and need additional help, contact us at contact@read2learn.net.

Watch Our SEO Videos For Free!

Do you learn faster by watching video?

If you want to watch our SEO videos for free, please take 60 seconds to post an honest review of this book. Your review will help us make improvements to the next edition of this book.

After you leave your review, send us an email (contact@read2learn.net) and we'll send you a link to watch our SEO videos for free.

"Become an SEO Noble"

I've created a private group limited to 20 people. In the group, I teach you advanced methods to accomplish everything in this book in less than 30 minutes per day.

In the group I reveal SEO trade secrets not openly discussed by anyone in the industry. I'll be your personal account manager, dedicate development hours to your website, and give you access to my resources to get everything done 100x faster.

Membership is by invitation only. Here are a few basic requirements:

- You must understand the basics presented in this book.
- Have your own product or service (no affiliate websites.)
- Minimum marketing budget of $600/month.
- Had your website for at least one year. (no new websites)

If you meet these requirements, request an invitation by sending me an email at contact@read2learn.net or request access here: https://elite.seonoble.org

I'll schedule a phone interview and if approved, you'll become an official member of the SEO Noble's. We'll get to work on your business right away and help you earn your first "noble rank" within the group.

Thank you for taking the time to read this short book, and I hope you do well with your business.

Kent Mauresmo & Anastasiya Petrova
https://SEOCompanyLosAngeles.us
https://elite.seonoble.org

SEO PDF Book:

https://seocompanylosangeles.us/seopdf

Additional Products by Read2Learn.net

"How To Build a Website With WordPress…Fast! [3rd Edition]"

"WordPress Web Hosting:
How to Use cPanel and Your Hosting Control Center"

"Book Publishing Blueprint:
How to Self Publish & Market Your Books…Fast!"